Law Enforcement Slogans

A Commitment To First Nations
A Force For Good
A Force For Your Safety
A Member Of The Home Team
A Safer North Wales
A Saga Of Sacrifice And Courage
Ahead, Always Ahead
Always At Your Service
Always Ready
An Honor To Serve, A Duty To Protect
At The Frontline Against Violent Crime

Dakota Ojibway Police Service, Manitoba, Canada
Sierra Leone Police
Romanian Gendarmerie
Singapore Police Force
North Wales Police
Jammu & Kashmir Police, India
Maldives National Defence Force
Assam Police, India
Pentagon Force Protection Agency, USA
Colorado State Patrol, USA
Bureau Of Alcohol, Tobacco, Firearms And Explosives, USA

Be Safe, Feel Safe
Better Out
Beyond The Call
Born Ready
Building Safer Communities Together

Cheshire Constabulary, England
Swedish Prison And Probation Service
Vancouver Police Department, Canada
United States Coast Guard
Devon & Cornwall Police, England

Caring and Protecting
Changing Lives, Protecting Canadians
Citizens First
Commitment And Excellence
Commitment Leadership Trust
Commitment To Combating Organized Crime
Committed To A Safer Dorset For You
Committed To Serve
Communicating, Facilitating, Regulating
Comprehensive Law Enforcement Services For A Safer New Mexico
Connecting Police For A Safer World
Contributing To A Safer Ohio
Courage Integrity Service
Courtesy, Loyalty, Service
Courtesy, Service And Protection Since 1935
Courtesy, Service, Excellence
Courtesy, Service, Protection
Creating A Better Place
Creating A Safe And Secure Malawi
Creating A Safer Cambridgeshire

Dumfries And Galloway Constabulary
Correctional Service Of Canada
Delhi Police, India
Customs And Excise Department, Hong Kong SAR, China
Lebanon Internal Security Forces
Federal Investigation Agency, Pakistan
Dorset Police, England
Rajasthan Police, India
Australian Communications And Media Authority
New Mexico State Police, USA
International Criminal Police Organization
Ohio State Highway Patrol, USA
Port Moody Police Department, Canada
Louisiana State Police, USA
Alabama Department Of Public Safety, USA
City Traffic Police Lahore, Pakistan
Kansas Highway Patrol, USA
Environment Agency, UK
Malawi Police Service
Cambridgeshire Constabulary, England

Dedicated To A Safe, Inclusive And Harmonious Community
Dedicated To Protect, Proud To Serve
Dedication, Enforcement, Coordination
Deeds Not Words
Defending Our Nation. Securing The Future
Delivering A Safer Victoria
Duty Unto Death

Regina Police Service, Canada
Edmonton Police Service, Canada
Narcotics Control Bureau, India
London Police Service, Canada
National Security Agency/Central Security Service, USA
Victoria Police, Australia
Border Security Force, India

Excellence In Service Through Quality Policing
Excellence, Duty, Truth

Timmins Police Service, Canada
Canadian Forces National Investigation Service

Fidelity, Bravery, Integrity
Fighting Crime, Protecting Communities
Fighting Crime, Protecting The Public
For The Good Of The Public
For The Law And For The People
For Your Safety And Security
For Your Safety. Your National Police

Federal Bureau Of Investigation, USA
Merseyside Police, England
Bedfordshire Police, England
Nebraska State Patrol, USA
National Republican Guard Portugal
Malta Police Force
Liechtenstein National Police Force

Gold in Peace, Iron in War

San Francisco Police Department, USA

Help And Cooperation
Helping Secure Australia's Future
High Quality, Fairness And Willingness To Cooperate
Hong Kong Our Advantage Is You And The ICAC
Honor, Duty, Fidelity
Honouring Each One's Uniqueness And The Creator's Gifts With Dignity And Respect
Human Rights, Efficiency, Discipline And Image
Humility Bravery Respect Wisdom Truth Love Honesty

International Security Assistance Force, Afghanistan
Australian Security Intelligence Organisation
National Traffic Police, Finland
Independent Commission Against Corruption, Hong Kong, China
New Jersey State Police, USA
Anishinabek Police Service, Canada
National Police Agency, Taiwan
Nishnawbe-Aski Police Service, Canada

In Cooperation We Create Security
Industry, Impartiality, Integrity
Integrity, Impartiality, Dignity
Integrity, Service, Pride
Integrity, Service, Professionalism

Estonian Police And Border Guard Board
Central Bureau Of Investigation, India
Burundi National Police
Illinois State Police, USA
Indiana State Police, USA

Justice, Integrity, Service

United States Marshals Service

Keeping Our Communities Safe
Keeping SA Safe
Keeping South Wales Safe

Grampian Police, Scotland
South Australia Police, Australia
South Wales Police

Law Makes Our Land Habitable
Leading And Partnering In Our Community To Serve And Protect
Leading Our Community Towards A Safer Tomorrow

Icelandic Police
Halifax Regional Police, Canada
City Of Kawartha Lakes Police Service, Canada

Making A Difference
Making Bermuda Safer
Making Jersey Safer

Tayside Police, England
Bermuda Police Service
States Of Jersey Police

One Team, One Goal: Your Safety
Our Priority Is You

Abu Dhabi Police, Abu Dhabi Emirate, UAE
Norfolk Constabulary, England

Partner In Progress
Partners For A Safe And Healthy Community
Peace Keeper Of The Nation
Peace, Justice, Service
Peace, Security, Commitment
People First Policing
People Serving People
Personal, Professional, Protective Policing
Police And Communities Together
Police To Its Last Particle Is Duty
Policing For You
Policing In Partnership
Policing With Pride
Preserving Our Freedoms, Protecting America
Pride In Service
Progress And Independence
Protect And Serve
Protecting And Promoting Your Health
Protecting And Reassuring
Protecting And Serving The People Of Kent
Protecting Communities And Targeting Criminals
Protecting National Security And Upholding Public Safety
Protecting Our Communities
Protecting Society & Reducing Crime
Protecting The Lives, Property & Constitutional Rights Of People In Idaho Since 1919
Protecting The Righteous & Controlling & Annihilating The Evil
Protection And Security
Protection, Service, Integrity
Public Safety In Partnership With Our Community
Putting Communities First
Putting People First

Federal Board Of Revenue, Pakistan
Brockville Police Service, Ontario, Canada
Central Reserve Police Force, India
Goa Police, India
Armed Police Force, Nepal
Gloucestershire Constabulary, England
Sarnia Police Service, Canada
Police Service Of Northern Ireland
Lancashire Constabulary, England
Punjab Police, India
Nottinghamshire Police, England
Pembroke Police Service, Canada
Lincolnshire Police, England
Department Of Homeland Security, USA
Islamabad Capital Territory Police, Pakistan
Opaskwayak Cree Nation Police Department, Canada
Uganda Police
U.S. Food And Drug Administration
Gwent Police, Wales
Kent Police, England
Humberside Police, England
U.S. Immigration And Customs Enforcement
Leicestershire Constabulary, England
Federal Bureau Of Prisons, USA
Idaho State Police, USA
Maharashtra Police, India
Central Industrial Security Force, India
Canada Border Services Agency
Brantford Police Service, Canada
Northamptonshire Police, England
Cleveland Police, England

Reach Home Safely - We Care For You

Jammu & Kashmir Traffic Police, India

Safe Communities, A Secure Ontario
Safe Skies For All
Safe, Satisfied And Confident Communities
Safeguarding Our Community
Safely Linking Communities
Safer Communities Together
Safer, Stronger Cumbria
Safety, Service And Security
Safety, Service, Friendship
Secure Borders For The Benefit Of The European Community
Securing A Safer Community
Securing America's Borders
Security, Service, Sacrifice
Selfless Service, Integrity, Responsibility
Service To All
Service With Humility
Service With Integrity
Service, Courage, Friendship
Service, Honor And Justice
Service, Protection, Integrity
Service, Security And Cooperation
Serving Our Communities, Protecting Them From Harm
Serving Sussex
Serving With A Smile
Serving With Pride And Distinction Since 1935
Serving, Protecting, Making The Difference
Simplifying What Is Legal, Preventing What Is Illegal
Soft In Temperament, Firm In Action
Strength Through Community

Ontario Provincial Police, Canada
Australian Civil Aviation Safety Authority
Wiltshire Constabulary, England
Dyfed-Powys Police, Wales
South Coast British Columbia Transportation Authority Police Service, Canada
New Zealand Police
Cumbria Constabulary, England
California Highway Patrol, USA
New Westminster Police Service, British Columbia, Canada
Romanian Border Police
Royal Papua New Guinea Constabulary
U.S. Customs And Border Protection
Nagaland Police, India
South Carolina Highway Patrol, USA
Kenya Police
Washington State Patrol, USA
Ghana Police
Tripura Police, India
Philippine National Police
Rwanda National Police
Haryana Police, India
West Midlands Police, England
Sussex Police, England
Puducherry Police, India
Arkansas State Police, USA
West Mercia Police, England
Swedish Customs Service
Kerala Police, India
Central Saanich Police Service, Canada

Taking Policing Closer To The Community
Taking Pride In Keeping Suffolk Safe
The Police Is In The Service Of The People
The Police Is Your Friend
The Well Being Of The People Is In The Supreme Law
To Be Globally Recognized As A Pioneer Of Customs Services
To Defend. To Protect. To Help
To Ensure The Safety & Security Of The People Of Fiji And Its Visitors
To Ensure The Safety And Security For Each Person In Our Community
To Help And To Protect
To Make Bhutan The Safest Place To Live And Work In South Asia
To Protect And Serve
To Protect And Serve With P.R.I.D.E
To Protect And To Serve
To Protect The Good And To Restrain The Evil
To Protect, Serve, And Reassure
To Provide A Policing Service That Is Uniquely St'at'imc
To Seek Justice, Preserve Peace And Improve The Quality Of Life For All
Together For A Safer Community
Together For Safer Communities
Together We Make A Difference
Together We Work For The Nation
Total Policing
Toward Safer Communities
Trust, Integrity And Communication: Your Voice At The National Level
Truth Alone Triumphs

Fife Constabulary, Scotland
Suffolk Constabulary, England
Sudan Police
Nigeria Police
Mauritius Police Force
Customs Affairs, Kingdom Of Bahrain
Lithuanian Police
Fiji Police Force
Phoenix Police Department, Texas USA
Police Of The Czech Republic
Royal Bhutan Police
Maldives Police Service
Trinidad And Tobago Police Service
Los Angeles Police Department, USA
Mumbai Police, India
Royal Barbados Police Force
Stl'atl'imx Tribal Police Service, Canada
Pennsylvania State Police, USA
Albanian State Police
Central Scotland Police
Moose Jaw Police Service, Canada
Directorate Of Revenue Intelligence, India
Northumbria Police, England
Pennsylvania Board Of Probation And Parole, USA
Association Of Law Enforcement Intelligence Units
Tamil Nadu Police, India

Unite The Fight Against Nationally Significant Crime
Unity, Responsibility, Loyalty

Australian Crime Commission
Niagara Regional Police Service, Canada

Valour - Steadfastness and Commitment

Indo-Tibetan Border Police, India

We Are Your Partners In Voluntary Compliance!
We Care For You
We Care, We Listen And We Act
We Ensure A Fair And Effective Financing Of The Future Public Sector
We Serve With Pride And Care
With Honour We Serve
With You, Making Surrey Safer
With Your Help, A Safer Community
Working For Safer Communities
Working In Partnership To Make Our Community Safer
Working In Partnership With The Community For A Safer Police
Working Together For A Safer Bahamas
Working Together To Maintain A Safe Community
Working Together To Make A Safer Community
Working With Communities To Protect And Serve

State Revenue Service, Latvia
Kolkata Police, India
Royal Cayman Islands Police Service
Danish Tax Authority
Hong Kong Police Force
Queensland Police Service, Australia
Surrey Police, England
New South Wales Police Force, Australia
Hampshire Constabulary, England
Thames Valley Police, England
Belize Police Department
Royal Bahamas Police Force
Royal Gibraltar Police
Ottawa Police Service, Canada
National Police Service Of Ireland

You And The Dryden Police Service Working Together To Prevent Crime
Your Safety Is Our Goal

Dryden Police Service, Canada
Namibian Police Force

Zero Deaths. Everyone Counts

Alaska Bureau Of Highway Patrol, USA

Law Enforcement Slogans was first shown in 2011 as a printed spreedsheet, forming part of the group show *What*, taking place in a disused London office.

The following year the work was shown in *The London Open* at the Whitechapel Gallery as a randomly ordered list in a single floor to ceiling column 2 metres wide, 6 metres high. A similar format for the work was used at the Herzliya Museum of Contemporary Art in the 2013 exhibition *Other People's Problems: Conflicts and Paradoxes*.

Chris Coombes was born in Germany in 1974 and received a BA and MA in Fine Art from Chelsea College of Art & Design, University of the Arts London, in 1998 and 2010 respectively. © 2013 Chris Coombes. All rights reserved. www.chriscoombes.cc

www.ingramcontent.com/pod-product-compliance
Lightning Source LLC
Chambersburg PA
CBHW051822170526
45167CB00005B/2123